DRAW DINOSAURS!

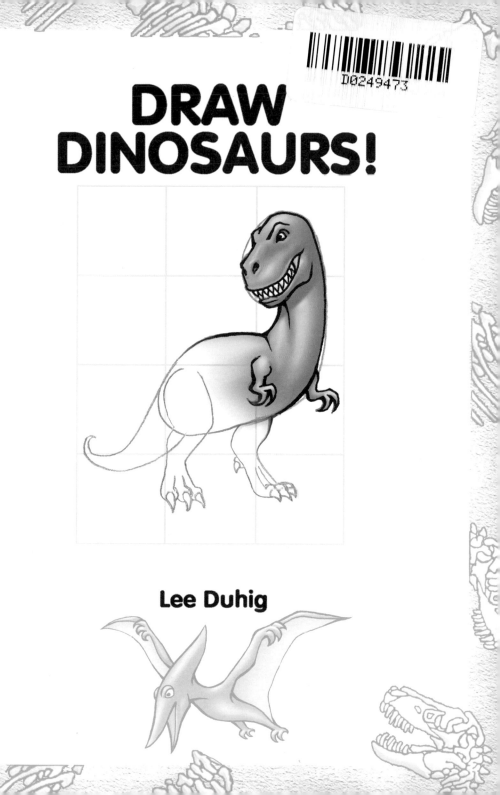

Lee Duhig

Draw Dinosaurs

Written & illustrated by
Lee Duhig

© 2006 by Mud Puddle Books, Inc.

Published by
Mud Puddle Books, Inc.
54 W. 21st Street
Suite 601
New York, NY 10010

info@mudpuddlebooks.com

ISBN: 1-59412-158-3

Printed in China.

Contents

INTRODUCTION:

Drawing is a fun and rewarding activity that can be enjoyed by all ages and can be done almost anywhere!

This book will show you how to draw the prehistoric animals known as dinosaurs in a few easy-to-follow steps!

You only need a few things to get started. They are:

A pencil with either a B or HB lead
These leads are soft and perfect for drawing.

An inking pen
Make sure the tip is thin so you can ink fine lines.

Colored pencils
Try to get as many colors as you can.

A soft white eraser
You should use this type, since erasers on the end of pencils are usually hard and smudge the pencil lines on the paper.

However, you really only need a pencil to get drawing, so don't worry if you don't have any of the other materials on hand!

4

How to use this book:

This book is set up in a simple, easy-to-follow way. Here are the steps:

1. We start with a simple squared grid. Draw some basic body shapes within the grid.

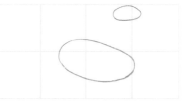

2. Connect the shapes together.

3. Add more shapes to define the subject.

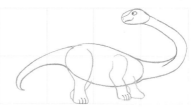

4. Then add details to finish the subject.

5. Finally, ink the figure with a pen. Then color the figure!

5

The current steps are shown in orange pencil to indicate what you are actively drawing. The previous steps are shown in blue pencil.

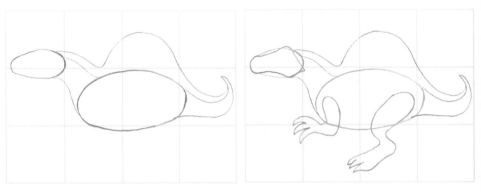

Don't feel you have to color the dinosaurs the way they are done in this book. They're just meant to show you one possible way to color them.
No one really knows what color dinosaurs were, so feel free to color them any way you like! Use your imagination!

6

Tiktaalik

A recent discovery that's 383-million years old, tiktaalik (which means "large shallow-water fish"), provides a link between fish and land animals. Tiktaalik was approximately 9-feet (3 m) long and could clearly function on both land and sea. It's jokingly referred to as a "fishapod". It had scales and gills but, unlike fish, it also had a neck, bones that suggest the beginnings of a wrist and fingers, and a large rib cage capable of supporting lungs. Fossils were discovered in the Canadian Arctic in 1994.

1. Draw a grid with 4 squares going across and 2 down.

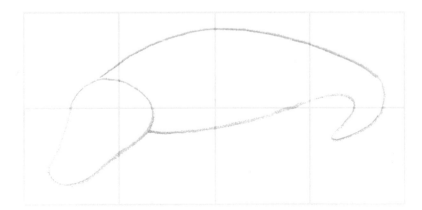

Draw a rounded cone shape on the right side of the grid.

Next, draw a rounded, stretched shape that gets smaller and curves around at the end.

7

2.

Next, draw in 2 rounded flippers on on the top and bottom where the 2 shapes from step 1 meet.

Add another flipper shape on the end of the curved, rounded end of the large shape from step 1.

3.

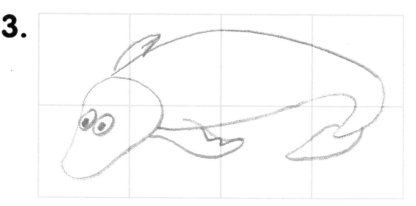

Draw 2 eyes very close together in the middle of the head.

On the 2 front flippers, draw 2 "W" shapes to define the "hands."

8

4. Now you can ink the shapes together using your pen, then erase the grid and any excess pencil lines.

5. Now you can color the dino GREEN using either colored pencils or markers.
Remember, the top of the dino will be a brighter shade of color.

You can also add water to show the dino coming out of the water onto land.

Dimetrodon

Not a dinosaur, dimetrodon was actually a pelycosaur, a large, primitive creature that lived millions of years before the dinosaurs. A gigantic carnivore (meat-eater), it had characteristics of mammals and reptiles. Its formidable jaw contained two types of teeth, hence its name, which means "two-measures tooth". Its legs sprawled from its sides, unlike dinosaurs, whose legs were underneath their bodies. The large sail on its back, which is actually a large flap of skin supported by bony spines and is characteristic of pelycosaurs, probably helped to regulate body temperature. Fossils have been found in Texas and Oklahoma.

1. Draw a grid with 4 squares going across and 2 down.

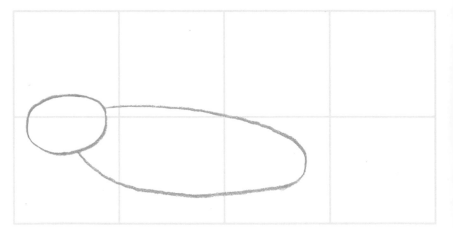

Draw 2 ovals: 1 small oval in the center on the left side of the grid, and another long, stretched oval on the right side of the smaller oval.

2.

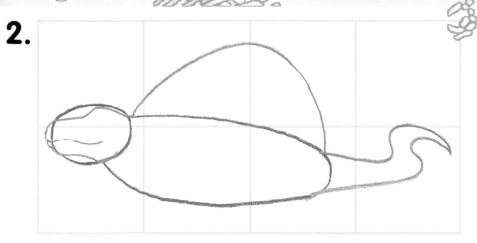

In the small oval, draw in the lines of the head and make the snout extend past the oval.
Next, draw a large, rounded curve above the stretched oval.
Then, draw some S-shaped curved lines to make the tail.

3.

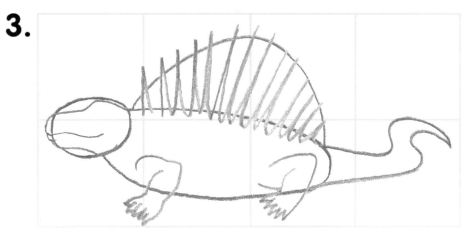

Draw in the legs of the dino and give it short, pointy toes.
Then, on top of the stretched oval, draw some long, sharp, spines that follow the curved line you drew in step 2.

4. Now you can draw in the nostril and eyeball. To finish the drawing, add rounded "W" shapes on top of the spines that follow the curve above the dino's back.

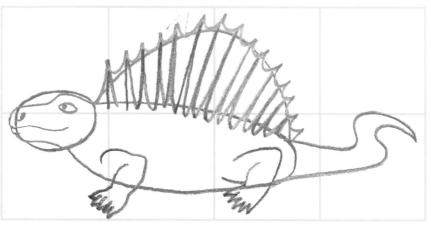

5. Ink the dino and erase the grid.

Color the body of the dino a BROWNISH GREEN and its belly a TAN color.

Make the webbing between the spines a DARK YELLOW.

Velociraptor

An extremely fast, two-legged meat-eater with a large brain and 80 very sharp, curved teeth, velociraptor stood about 3 feet (1 m) tall. One of the smartest dinosaurs, velociraptor probably hunted in packs that were capable of taking down much larger animals. Dinner was likely to be anything that crossed its path. Its slender legs could sprint up to 40 mph (60 km/hr). It likely had the ability to jump. Fossils were first discovered in Mongolia in 1924.

1. Draw a grid with 3 squares going across and 3 down.

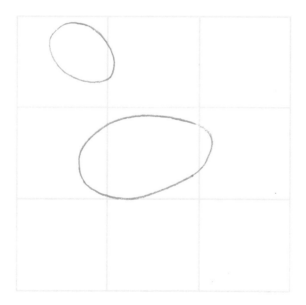

Draw 2 shapes: an oval shape in the center of the grid, and an "egg" shape in the upper left corner of the grid.

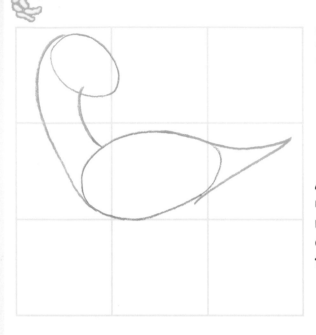

2.
Draw 2 curved lines from the circle to the oval shape.

Add 2 lines curving upward from the right side of the center oval shape to make the tail.

3. Within the "egg" shape, draw the lines of the head. Add the brow, snout and jaw.

Draw the shape of the arms and the 2 legs of the dino. Give the dino rounded toes and fingers.

14

4.

Draw the eyeball, nostril, and curve of the mouth.

Add a neck curve line to show the neck twisting.

Draw 3 claws on each hand.

Last, draw 3 claws on the feet, but make the inner claws at least three times the size of the other toe claws.

5. Ink your dino and erase the grid.

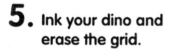

Color your dino a REDDISH PINK.

Make the eye a BRIGHT YELLOW.

15

Spinosaurus

This "spiny lizard" is now thought to be the largest land carnivore in history, 50 feet (15 m) in length and weighing up to 8 tons. All this weight was carried on two legs, although its two longish "arms" may have allowed it to walk on all fours at times. Fossils were first described and named in 1915 in Africa. These were lost in World War II, and it was only a recent discovery of a Spinosaurus skull that allowed the creature to take its rightful place in the dinosaur pantheon. Fossils have been found in Northern Africa and Argentina.

1. Draw a grid with 4 squares going across and 3 down.

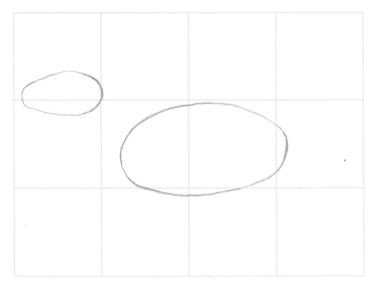

Draw 2 ovals: 1 large one in the center of the grid, and a small one toward the left upper corner of the grid.

2.

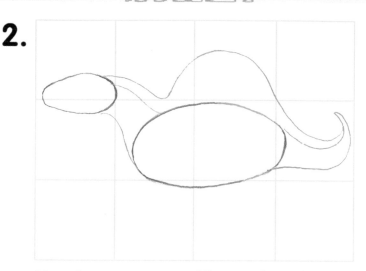

Now draw some curved lines to form the neck and tail.
Above those lines, draw another curved line that follows the neck, arcs up high above the body oval, then sweeps downward into the tail lines.

3.

Draw in the shape of the head in the small oval.
Give the back of the jaw a triangular point.
Next, draw the arm and leg of the dino.

4.

On the curved line above the neck and body, draw rounded humps and lines to make the spines. Next, draw in the eye socket, eyeball, and a curvy mouth.

Draw curved shapes to separate the claws.

5. Finish by inking the drawing and erasing the grid.

Color the dino a
DARK BROWNISH-TAN
and the spines a
DARK TAN.

Make the underside of
the dino a lighter shade.

18

Tyrannosaurus Rex

Perhaps the most famous dinosaur of all, the T-Rex was a huge, fierce, meat-eating predator whose fossils have been found in Mongolia and western North America. This 40-foot (12 m)-long creature was up to 20 feet (6 m) tall and, like many dinosaurs, walked on its toes! Within its 4-foot (1 m)-long jaw were 60 thick teeth that could easily pulverize bone. If its teeth were lost or damaged, T-Rex could grow new ones. Given its tremendous size and weight, the T-Rex was surprisingly agile and fast-moving. T-Rex translates as "tyrant lizard king".

1. Draw a grid with 3 squares going across and 4 down.

Draw 2 ovals: 1 in the middle of the grid, the other toward the upper right corner of the grid.

19

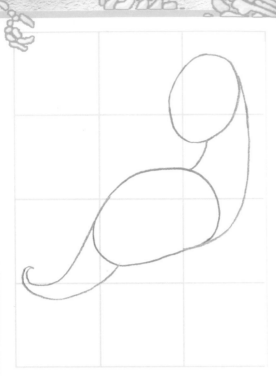

2.

Draw in 2 curved lines to connect the 2 shapes.

Next, draw the curved lines of the tail on the left side of the center oval.

3.

Define the head shape and add nostrils and eye sockets.

Draw a "wavy" curved line for the lower jaw.

Next, draw the legs and short arms of the dino.

Give the dino 2 hand claws and 3 foot claws.

4.

Draw in a dot for the eye, curved lip lines, and a set of sharp, pointy teeth.

Draw two short, vertical lines on the neck to show the neck twisting.

Finally, add the foot claws and foot details. Also, add a 4th claw underneath the right foot.

5. Ink your dino and erase the grid lines.

Color the dino a **DARK YELLOW-GREEN**.

Stegosaurus

The largest of the "armored dinosaurs", stegosaurus (the name means "covered lizard" or "roof lizard") had a brain about the size of a large nut, which is to say, it wasn't very smart. Two rows of bony plates ran along its back. While their use is unknown, they may have helped regulate the animal's temperature as well as protect the dinosaur against enemies. Stegosaurus was a toothless herbivore (it ate only plants). Fossils were first discovered in Colorado in 1876 and have since been found at sites all over the world.

1. Draw a grid with 4 squares going across and 3 down.

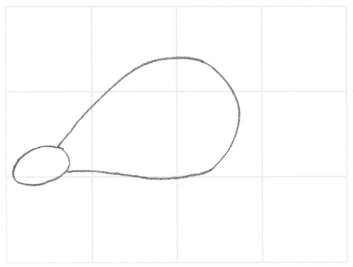

Draw 2 shapes: a small oval at the lower left center of the grid, and then a rounded "balloon" shape starting from the right of the small oval toward the center of the grid.

2.

On the right of the balloon shape, draw curved lines to form the tail.
Next, draw a short set of front legs and a large set of rear legs, each with 3 toes.

3.

In the small oval, draw the head detail.
Following the upper curve of the body and tail, draw a series of small to large triangular plates that end at the tail in 2 long, pointy spikes.

4. Draw in the nostril, dot for the eye, mouth line, and small curves to separate the claws from the feet.

Finally, draw upside-down V-shaped lines to show the triangular plates on the other side of the dino.

5. Ink the dinosaur and erase the grid. Color the dino's body GREEN on top and YELLOW on the bottom.

Make the triangular plates a REDDISH-BROWN color.

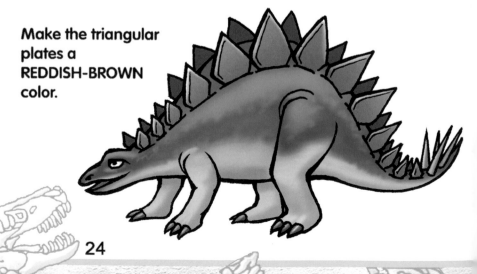

Triceratops

Along with the T-Rex, triceratops is one of the most famous of all dinosaurs. It belongs to a group of horned dinosaurs. With its armored plating, it looks like a distant cousin to the rhinoceros. It had three horns on its face and a parrot-like beak for a mouth. Triceratops may look formidable and fierce, but it was, in fact, a plant-eater living in great herds for protection. The four short legs meant that triceratops was slow-moving. It was a favorite food for T-Rex. Fossils were first discovered in Colorado in 1888 and have since been found in other sites in western Canada and the United States.

1. Draw a grid with 4 squares going across and 3 down.

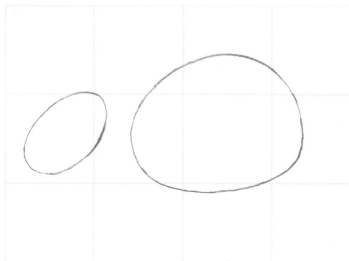

Draw 2 ovals: a large one to the right center of the grid, and then a smaller, egg-shaped one to the left center of the grid.

2.

Draw the curved lines of the neck to connect the 2 ovals.

Next, draw the curved lines for the tail.

Then draw the shapes for the legs.

3. On the egg-shaped oval, draw in the lines of the face. Make the mouth beak-like, like a parrot's.

Now draw in the large plate for the back of the head.

4.

Draw in the nostril and eyeball.

Now we'll draw in the horns: 1 on the snout, 2 jutting out from just above the eye, and 1 on the "cheek."

Draw in the toe claws and toes on the dino's feet.

5.

Ink your drawing and erase the grid.

Color the dino a GREENISH YELLOW with a PALE ORANGE underside.
Color the horns WHITE.

27

Compsognathus

About the size of a modern-day chicken, compsognathus (the name means "pretty jaw") is one of the smallest of known dinosaurs. It was speedy and quite agile, getting around on two pencil-thin legs capped by three-toed feet. Its small, pointed head sitting on a long, flexible neck featured a large mouth with an array of tiny but sharp teeth. Its two short arms helped it catch its diet of small animals and insects. A fossil was first discovered in the late 1850s in southern Germany. Later, a second fossil was excavated in France. To date, that's all that's been found.

1. Draw a grid with 4 squares going across and 3 down.

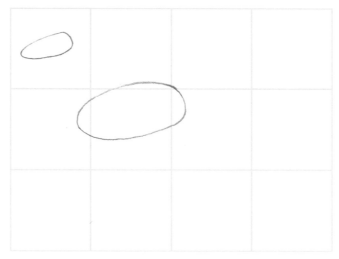

Draw two oval shapes: one to the left-center of the grid, the other smaller and in the top-left corner of the grid.

28

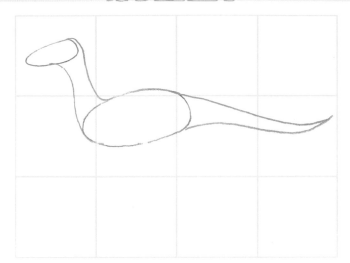

2. Connect the two shapes by drawing two curved lines between them to form the neck of the dino.
On the far right of the center oval, draw 2 curved lines for a long tail.

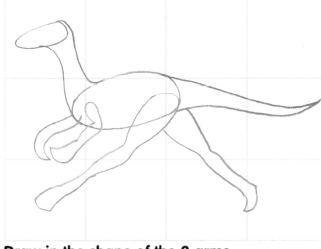

3. Draw in the shape of the 2 arms.

Next, draw in the shape of the 2 long legs. Spread the legs far apart to show that the dino is walking.

4. To finish the drawing, draw in the long mouth and round eyeball.
Then draw 2 curved claws for hands and draw in the 3-clawed feet. Add an additional claw to each foot on the heels of the dino.

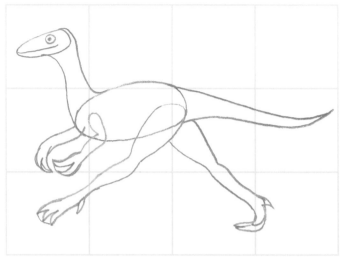

5. Ink your dino and erase the grid and pencil lines.

Color the dino a PALE TANNISH color. Add some DEEP BLUE color to the top of the head and wavy BLUE lines to the dino's upper body.

Iguanodon

A relative speed-demon among dinosaurs, iguanodon is thought to have lived in great herds. It ran on two legs and probably walked on four. Its short arms had four fingers and a spiked thumb useful in both finding food and fighting off predators. A plant-eater, it had a horny, toothless beak of a mouth that was packed with side teeth in its cheeks. Fossils were first found in 1822 in southern England. Since then, fossils have been found throughout the world, with the exception of Antarctica.

1. Draw a grid with 4 squares going across and 3 down.

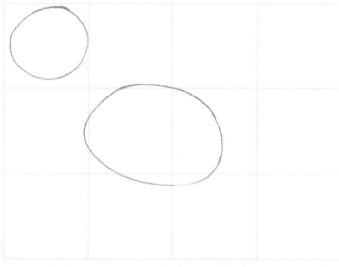

Draw 2 shapes: an oval shape in the center of the grid, and a circle in the upper left corner of the grid.

2.

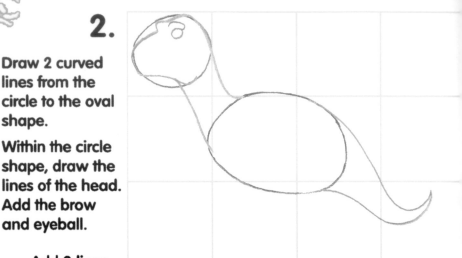

Draw 2 curved lines from the circle to the oval shape.

Within the circle shape, draw the lines of the head. Add the brow and eyeball.

Add 2 lines curving downward from the right side of the center oval shape to make the tail.

3. Draw the shape of the arms and the 2 legs of the dino.

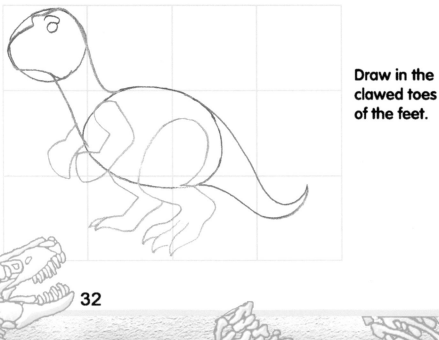

Draw in the clawed toes of the feet.

4.

Draw in the nostril, mouth, and dot for the eyeball.

Next, draw in the fingers on the hands. Give this dino 5 fingers.

Draw in some circular curves to separate the claws from the feet of the dino.

5. Ink in the dino and erase the grid.

Color the dino a PALE ORANGISH-BROWN.

Color the bottom of the dino a PALE TAN color.

33

Ankylosaurus

This huge (35-foot/11-m-long), fierce-looking, armored dinosaur was, in all probability, a big, gentle, not-too-bright plant-eater. It was covered in thick, bony plates and 2 rows of sharp spikes that offered ample protection from predators. If this weren't enough, its club-like tail could be a formidable weapon. Only its underbelly was vulnerable. In spite of its short legs, it was capable of running at a good clip. Fossils were first found in 1908 and have been recovered in Montana and Alberta, Canada. Tracks (which help determine the speed at which a dinosaur moved) have been found in Bolivia, South America.

1. Draw a grid with 3 squares going across and 3 down.

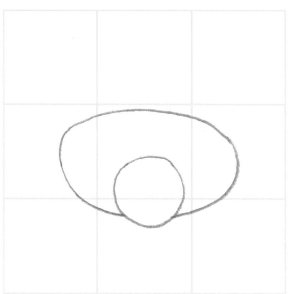

Draw 2 shapes in the center of the grid. One shape will be a circle, the other will be an oval drawn around the circle.

2.

On both sides of the oval shape, draw in 4 legs.

On the circle, draw a wide "V" for the mouth and 2 small circles for eyes.

Above the oval body, draw a circle with 2 curved lines under it.

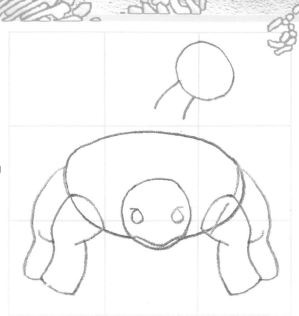

3.

Add a series of upside-down "V" shapes along the top of the oval body shape, following the curve of the oval. Make 4 more rows of these toward the head shape.

Next, add 3 curved lines inside the circle that you drew above the body.

Now, add 4 more V-shaped spikes on both sides of the dino's head.

35

4.

Add some more rows of smaller spikes to the tail of the dino.

Draw small, straight lines down the centers of all the spikes.

Add the toes and claws to the feet.

Last, add 2 circular nostrils in the middle of the head down toward the mouth, and add 2 dots in the eyes.

5.

Ink your dino and erase the grid.

COLOR the dino a DARK TAN.

COLOR the spikes a LIGHT TAN.

Shade the spikes light on one side and dark on the other side to make them more real!

Pteranodon

Not a dinosaur, but a flying reptile, pteranodon had a wingspread of up to 33 feet (10 m), wider than any known bird's. If it stood on its two legs, it would reach a height of 6 feet (2 m). Brainy—that is to say, they had large brains—with excellent eyesight, pteranodons were carnivores even though they had no teeth. They probably ate fish, shellfish, crabs, and insects as well as scavenged for dead animals on land. Some scientists believe they ate like pelicans, scooping their prey from the water and swallowing them whole. Fossils have been known since 1876 and have been found primarily in Kansas and England.

1. Draw a grid with 4 squares going across and 3 down.

Draw 2 shapes in the center of the grid.
Draw the larger shape toward the left of the center of the grid, Start by drawing the letter "W", and extend two lines upward to a point.

To the right of the 1st shape, draw a sideways "tear" shape.

37

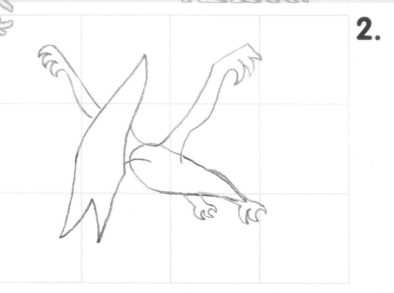

Next, draw 2 arms with 3 pointy fingers stretched in a "V" shape between the first 2 shapes.
Draw 2 curves, one inward one outward, to join the 2 shapes.
Next, on the pointy end of the "tear" shape, draw 2 clawed feet.

3.

Draw the wings of the dino and connect the bottom of the right wing to the right foot.

4.

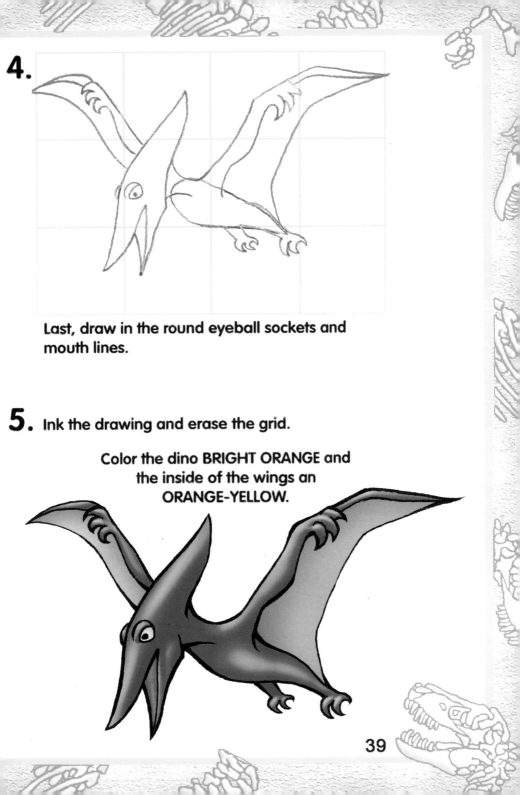

Last, draw in the round eyeball sockets and mouth lines.

5. Ink the drawing and erase the grid.

Color the dino BRIGHT ORANGE and the inside of the wings an ORANGE-YELLOW.

Dilong paradoxus

Newly discovered fossils in 2004 in northeastern China gave us our first glimpse at dilong paradoxus, a small feathered dinosaur that was a primitive relative of the gigantic T-Rex. These feathers were clearly for warmth, not flying, and many scientists are exploring the possibility that even large dinosaurs had feathers at some stage of their development, perhaps losing them as they matured. Many dinosaurs share characteristics of modern-day birds and, like birds, may have been warm-blooded, unlike cold-blooded reptiles. There is much research and study that still needs to be done. Dilong was 5 feet long (1.6 m) and, like the T-Rex, a meat-eater.

1. Draw a grid with 2 squares going across and 4 down.

Draw two oval-like shapes, one in the upper left corner of the grid, and another, larger one in the center of the grid.

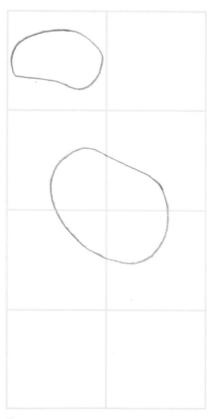

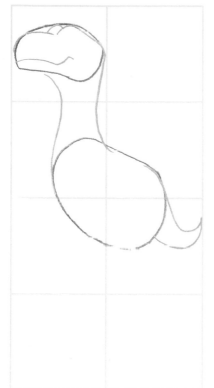

2.

Next, connect the 2 ovals using 2 curved lines.
Then do another set of curved lines that form a curved point on the right of the center oval.

Draw in the mouth lines and 2 rounded bumps on the top of the head.
Add a curve for the snout.

3.

Draw in the arms and the legs. Make sure to start them in the center of the body oval.
Give this dino 3 large, pointy fingers.

41

4.

Add some "zig-zag" strokes to show that this dino is furry. Draw these on the back of the dino's neck toward his head and on the top of the dino's tail.

Draw the curves on the hands and feet to separate the claws.

Add an additional claw on the back of the dino's left foot.

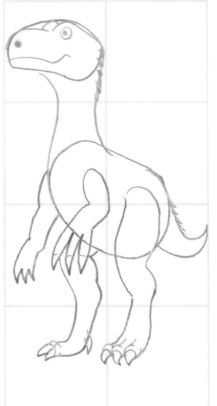

5.

Ink the dino with your pen and erase the grid.

Color the dino's head, hands, and feet PINK.

Color the dino's fur a DARK BLUISH-GREEN to a BRIGHT YELLOW to a BRIGHT ORANGE at the top.

42

Hagryphus giganteus

In 2005, scientists digging in southern Utah found the fossilized hands and feet of what turned out to be the remains of a new and rather bizarre looking feathered dinosaur. Named for the Egyptian god of the western desert (Ha) and a Greek mythological bird (griffin), hagryphus was an enormous, birdlike creature (10 feet/3 m long, 7 feet/2 m tall) that looked like a giant, technicolor turkey. Hagryphus had a toothless beak but strong arms and claws that allowed it to eat both meat and plants.

1. Draw a grid with 4 squares going across and 4 down.

Draw 3 shapes: a circle in the middle of the grid, an oval in the upper right of the grid, and a curved "fan" shape in the upper left of the grid.

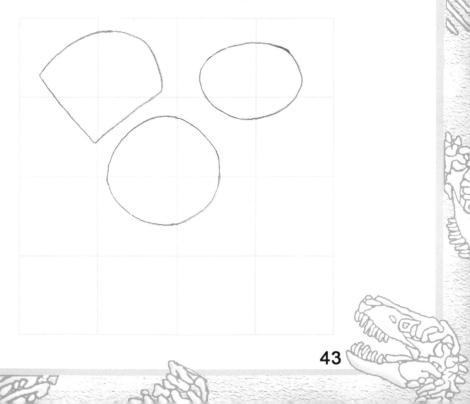

2.

Connect the fan shape to the center circle using 2 curved lines. Connect the oval to the center circle by making 2 wide, curved lines.

Draw in the arms and a curved "W" shape for the top of the legs.

Give this dino 2 rounded fingers.

3. Now, within the fan shape, add some long, wavy lines.

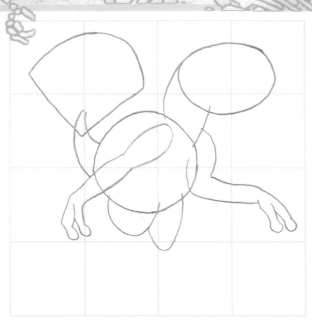

Add a row of feathers to the bottom of each arm.

Draw a series of curves within the head shape and add a slanted, rectangular shape to the top of the head.

Then, finish drawing the legs and feet.

4.

Add some "zig-zag" fur lines to the dino.

Add the details of the head, including the eye, pointy tongue, and nostril.

Now draw in the claws on the hands and feet.

Add a 4th claw to the back of the longer leg.

5.

Ink your drawing and erase the grid.

> Color the dino's body REDDISH-BROWN, but make the underside of the dino A GRAYISH-WHITE.

Make the head and under-arm feathers BLUE.

The hands, feet, beak, and rectangle shape above the head should be YELLOW.

The fan-shape at the end of the tail can be BROWN to WHITE to BLUE.

45

Guanlong wucaii

Early in 2006, scientists announced that fossils belonging
to the oldest (to date) relative of T-Rex had been discovered
in China's far northwest corner, near the Gobi Desert.
Named guanlong wucaii, meaning "crowned dragon
of the five-colored rocks", this creature had a spectacular,
multi-colored crest on its head. The crest is a bit of a mystery, since
it was too fragile to use for defense. Guanlong was about the
size of T-Rex. It was feathered like a chicken and a meat-eater with
long, sharp teeth. Its two long, powerful back legs would have allowed it to race about
swiftly. Its two shorter arms were capped by three fingers and long nails that were
ideal for slicing and dicing.

1. Draw a grid with 4 squares going
across and 3 down.

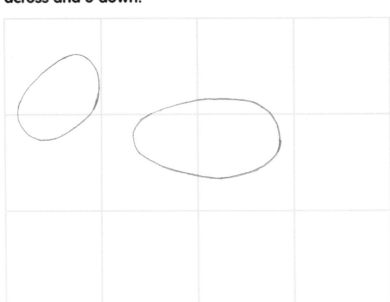

Draw 2 egg-shaped ovals: one in the upper
center of the grid and another, slightly smaller
one at an angle toward the upper left corner
of the grid.

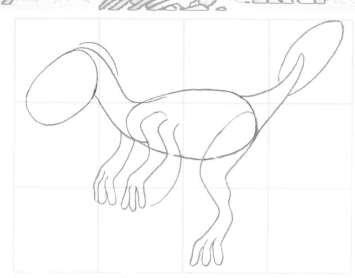

2. Draw a series of curved lines, 1 set for the neck, and another set to form the tail.
Draw an oval shape at the end of the tail shape.
Next, draw the curved lines for the arms and legs and round out the toes and fingers.

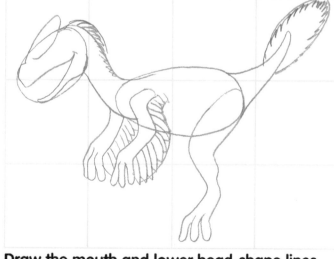

3. Draw the mouth and lower head-shape lines. Add an angled, oval shape to the head just above the mouth. Last, add "wavy" feather lines to the neck, under the arms, and around the oval shape at the end of the tail.

47

4. Now to finish the drawing.
Add 2 rows of tiny, pointed teeth.
Draw in the nostril and eyeball. Also add a curved line in the oval shape that you drew on top of the head.
Draw in the last leg and some pointy, triangle-shaped fingernails and toenails.

5.

Color the dino
a PINKISH TAN.

Add a large, PURPLE
patch to the back of the dino.

Make the oval shape on the
head a bright PINK.

Color the feathers under the
arms a GRAYISH PURPLE.

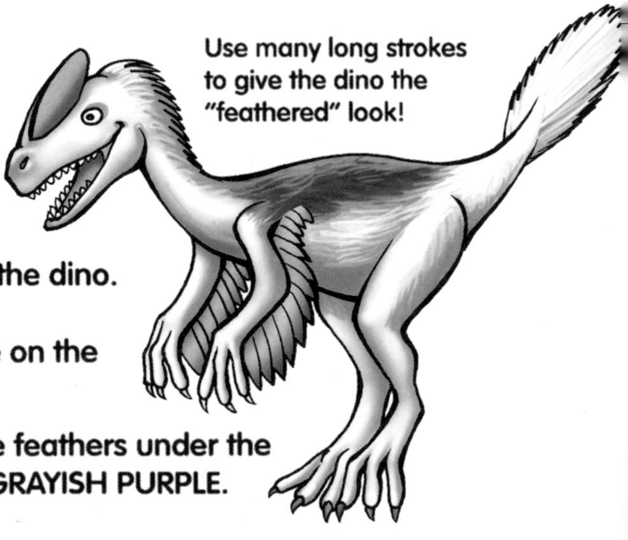

Use many long strokes
to give the dino the
"feathered" look!

48

Incisivosaurus gauthieri

Fossils belonging to one of the oddest-looking dinosaurs ever were found in northeast China in 2002. Incisivosaurus was about the size of a turkey, feathered and fast. It looked like a cross between the extinct dodo bird and a rabbit. The rodent-like, protruding front teeth probably meant that incisivosaurus was content to gnaw on plants, seeds and vegetables rather than meat. Like many modern birds, it swallowed pebbles to help grind up its food. This is one of many spectacular fossil discoveries that have come out of China in the last few years.

1.

Draw a grid with 3 squares going across and 4 down.

Then draw 2 circles: one toward the left center of the grid, and one slightly smaller one toward the top-right corner of the grid.

2.

Next, draw a whole bunch of curved lines to make the neck, tail, arms, legs, and mouth, plus a circle for the eye of our dino.

Give the arms and legs 3 pointy fingers and toes each, and draw the tail pointing upwards.

3.

Now add the wavy lines to give our dino feathers!

Add them to the back of the arms, down the neck, and on top of the body.

Also, add feathers to the top of the neck, ending at the top of the head.

Lastly, add a flame-like feather shape above the tail!

4.

Define the bumpy shape of the head and add an eyeball and nostril dot.

Add ring shapes to separate the fingernails from the hands and small curves to separate the toenails from the feet.

Draw in the curve of the mouth and give this dino 2 big "buckteeth."

5.

Ink the dino and erase the grid.

Color the body a TANNISH GRAY.

Color the face and feet YELLOW.

Color the feathers behind the arms and on the tail a DEEP BLUE.

51

Liaoceratops yanzigouensis

Another recent (2001) discovery from northeast China, lianoceratops is the oldest and smallest horned dinosaur found to date, a distant, primitive cousin to the gigantic triceratops. Lianoceratops, a plant-eater, was about the size of a large hare. Like other horned dinosaurs, it had a large (relative to its total size), bony protrusion behind its skull. Because of its lack of protection and its small size, lianoceratops was probably a favorite food of meat-eating dinosaurs. A discovery such as this provides a valuable link to understanding the evolution of dinosaurs.

1. Draw a grid with 4 squares going across and 3 down.

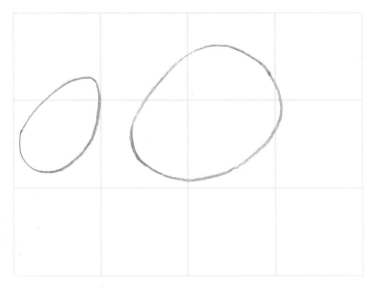

Draw 2 ovals: a large one in the upper center of the grid, and then a smaller, egg-shaped one toward the left side of the larger oval.

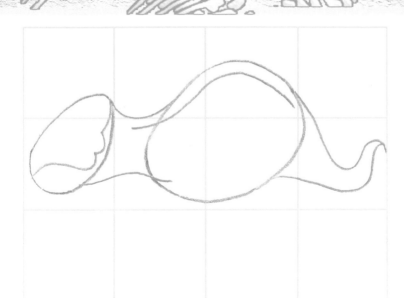

2. Draw some curved lines to connect the small oval to the large oval. Then add a curved line that follows the upper body to the neck. Add the curved tail and draw the shape of the lower head.

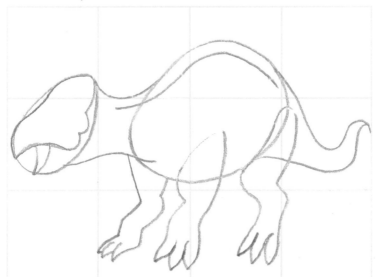

3. Draw the dip of the head, a curved triangle for the mouth, and then draw the legs and give the dino 3 pointy toes on each foot.

53

4.

Finish drawing the dino by adding the nose, round eye, 2 round "bumps" on the lower part of the head, and a pointy tongue.

Also, draw tiny curves to separate the toenails from the feet, and add a 4th toenail to the rear leg just above the other toes.

5. Ink your dino and erase your grid.

Color the dino an "earthy" TAN color.

Effigia okeeffeae

Excavations at the Ghost Ranch Quarry in New Mexico in 1947 and 1948 produced a treasure trove of fossils. This one sat in storage for nearly 60 years before it was studied, identified and named in 2006. Not really a dinosaur but an ancient ancestor of modern alligators and crocodiles, effigia walked about on two legs, was about six feet (2 m) long and completely toothless. It was named effigia, which means "ghost", because of the six decades it remained hidden in plain sight, and okeeffeae for the artist Georgia O'Keefe, who once lived near the excavation site.

1.

Draw a grid with 3 squares going across and 2 down.

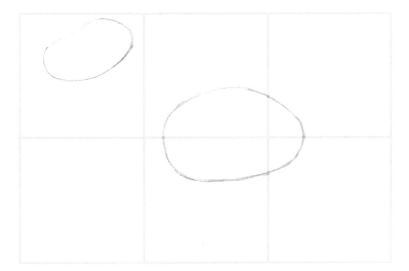

Begin with a bean-shaped oval in the top-left grid.

Next, draw an egg-shaped oval in the center grid facing toward the right.

2. **Next, connect the 2 ovals using 2 curved lines.**

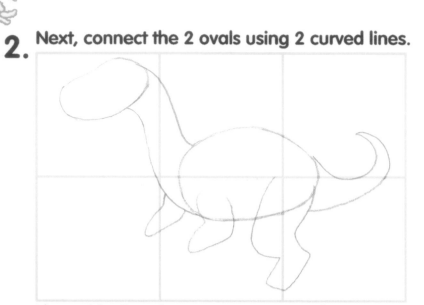

Then add 2 lines that connect to a curved point
at the end on the right of the "egg" shape.
Next, draw the stumps of the arms and leg.

3.

Draw in the mouth, the circle for the eyes, and
a dot for the nostril.
Next, draw in the pointy fingers and toes
and the remaining leg.

4. To finish the drawing, erase the connecting lines from step 2 so that the shapes become one whole, connected body.

Using your marker, ink over the pencil lines and erase the remaining pencil lines.

5. With your colored pencils, color the dinosaur green, with a reddish-pink mouth and an orange-yellow eye.

Erketu Ellisoni

Imagine putting a 24-foot (7 m)-long neck on a school bus and adding a 12-foot (4 m)-long tail. This would give you an idea of the size of erketu ellisoni, which was actually a modest-sized sauropod. Sauropods were semi-aquatic, four-legged, plant-eating dinosaurs with incredibly long necks that were among the largest living creatures ever. Erketu, like other sauropods, probably strolled with its neck and head parallel to the ground. Still, it's hard to imagine how they walked without falling flat on their faces. Erketu fossils were first found in 2002 in the Gobi Desert of Mongolia.

1. Draw a grid with 4 squares going across and 2 down.

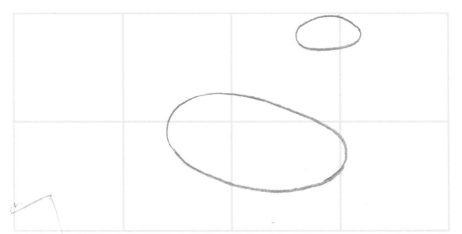

Draw 2 ovals: one large one in the center of the grid, and one smaller one at the top of the grid toward the right of the 1st oval.

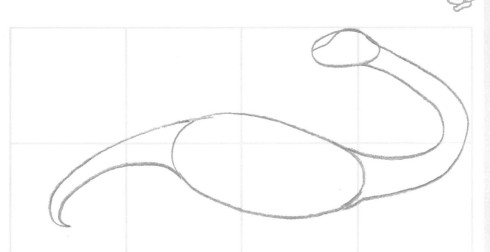

2. Draw 2 lines to the left of the large oval and have them curve downward and meet at a point. Next, draw 2 more lines that curve toward the head oval, then draw the dip of the head.

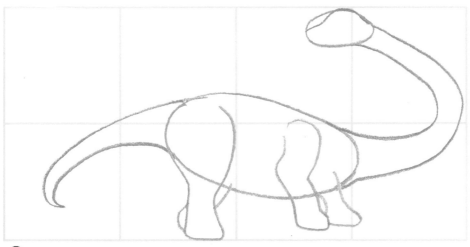

3. On the large oval, draw in the legs and feet, which are shaped sort of like thick chicken drumsticks.

4. On the feet, draw tiny curves to make toes.

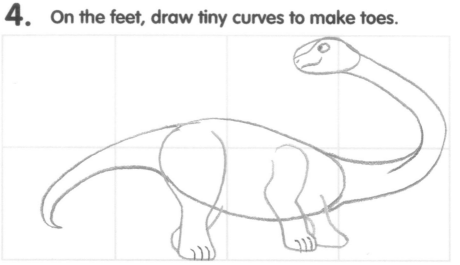

On the head, add an eye, mouth and dot for the nostril.
Last, add a curved "neck-bend" line at
the middle of the long neck.

5. Ink the dino and erase
the grid.

Color the dino a grassy GREEN!

Castorocauda lutrasimilis

Not a dinosaur, but a mammal-like creature that lived among the dinosaurs, castorocauda was a furry, fish-eating swimmer who lived in burrows more than 160 million years ago. Its fossil remains, intact with fur, were found in Inner Mongolia in 2004. It had a body like an otter, teeth like a seal, webbed hind feet like a platypus, and a flat tail like a beaver. Although it was only about a foot and a half (46 cm) long, it's the largest mammal-like animal of its time and offers the first evidence of a land animal adapting to the water. When its discovery was announced, a startled press quickly nicknamed it the "Jurassic beaver".

1. Draw a grid with 3 squares going across and 2 down.

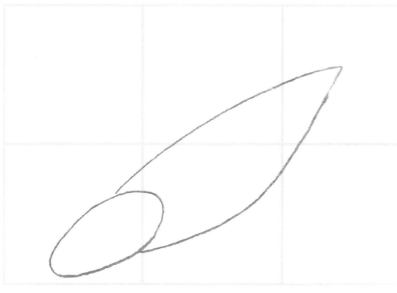

Next, draw a stretched oval in the bottom-left grid, then add a large "fin" shape to make the body. Make the shape point toward the upper right of the grid.

61

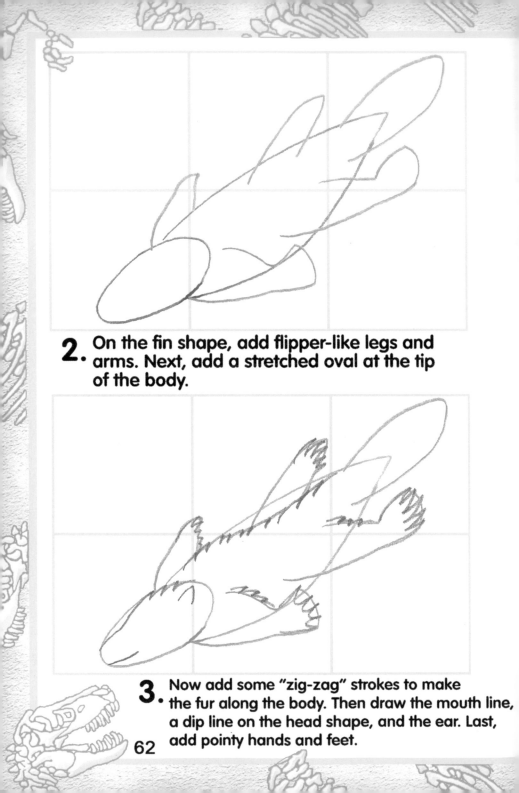

2. On the fin shape, add flipper-like legs and arms. Next, add a stretched oval at the tip of the body.

3. Now add some "zig-zag" strokes to make the fur along the body. Then draw the mouth line, a dip line on the head shape, and the ear. Last, add pointy hands and feet.

62

4.

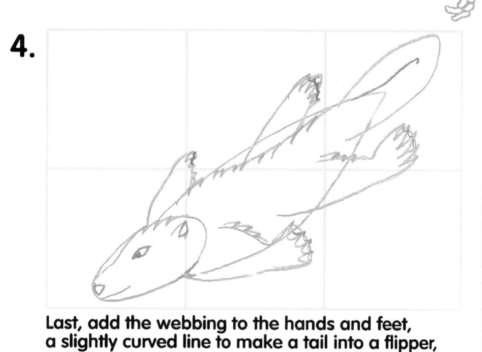

Last, add the webbing to the hands and feet,
a slightly curved line to make a tail into a flipper,
and the triangular nose and inner ear.
Also, give our dino an eye!

5. Ink the final drawing and erase the grid.

Color the dino BROWN to
LIGHT TAN and give the it
some broad, "furry" strokes!

You can also add
water to the
background
if you like!

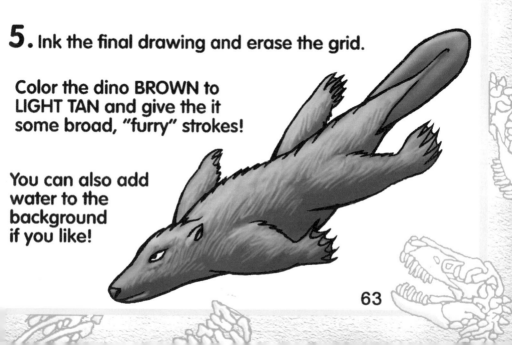

63

Index